ALTERNATE ASSESSMENT
IN THE SCIENCE CLASSROOM

GLENCOE
McGraw-Hill

New York, New York   Columbus, Ohio   Mission Hills, California   Peoria, Illinois

Send all inquiries to:
Glencoe/McGraw-Hill
936 Eastwind Drive
Westerville, Ohio 43081

ISBN 0-02-826429-0

Printed in the United States of America.

13 14 15 16 17 18   066   02 01 00 99 98 97

Alternate Assessment in the Science Classroom

Table of Contents

THE NEED FOR ALTERNATE ASSESSMENT

Introduction

As a teacher of science, you know only too well the demands of your job. Preparing for class, motivating students, maintaining order in the classroom, teaching, grading papers, and handling other school duties are only some of the tasks you face each day. Professional journals and the news media, curriculum consultants, speakers at conferences, fellow faculty members, and even neighbors and friends discuss changes in the science curriculum—and you feel the pressure to keep up with the new developments. Improving instruction and learning becomes a continuous and demanding process that requires a great deal of hard work on the part of every teacher of science.

Today, the school science curriculum is changing again, and, as it changes, there is a growing need for alternate assessment. Two major national efforts, the National Science Teachers Association (NSTA) Project on Scope, Sequence, and Coordination (SS&C) and the American Association for the Advancement of Science (AAAS) Project 2061, are involved along with the National Research Council in the extensive restructuring of K-12 science education. All of these restructuring programs incorporate assessment methods that go far beyond traditional paper-and-pencil content testing. The purpose of this booklet is to discuss how the curriculum is changing and what assessment methods are needed to monitor and measure the performance of students in the restructured science curriculum.

The Recent Past

During the past thirty years, starting with the science curriculum reform movement that began in the late 1950's, there have been numerous curriculum development projects funded by the National Science Foundation and other interested organizations. These projects covered all science disciplines and all grade levels. Some were focused within a single science discipline while others were interdisciplinary. What emerged from this period of reform and experimentation was a large bank of well-written and field-tested laboratory activities organized around various conceptual and process-skill frameworks.

In the 1980's, the science education community took a critical look at these curriculum projects and their effects on textbooks, instruction, and student achievement. The quality of the activities was high, but there were concerns about implementation, overall goals, coordination, and integration of the various curricula. Additionally, broad-based assessment data indicated problems with the performance of students in United States' schools and the measures used to assess this performance. These concerns led to the current restructuring movement in science education.

The major science education restructuring efforts go beyond the curriculum development projects of the past. While SS&C and Project 2061 still emphasize hands-on learning experiences, they take a broader and deeper philosophical view on how students learn science. Between them, they investigate content sequencing, student preconceptions, design issues, the role of materials, the role of history, the integration and coordination of the sciences, and the relevance of science to the everyday lives of students. A major element of both of these projects and the emerging National Science Education Standards being developed by the National Research Council is a thorough analysis and investigation of alternate assessment methods.

New Jobs Require New Skills

Ultimately, all students leave school at some level and are confronted with the prospect of finding a job. The demands of a job and the skills of a person seeking it must be compatible before an employer will match the two. The requisite skills for living and working in today's world and the world of tomorrow are learned in school. The curriculum is the primary instrument for teaching students the skills they will need to live productive and successful lives as citizens of the future.

A quick survey of our occupational landscape reveals that vast numbers of manufacturing jobs are leaving the United States for foreign countries. Years ago, people could hold their jobs with an elementary school education. But such an education today is inadequate because the jobs don't exist. Another view of the landscape reveals that many of today's jobs are completely new; that is, they didn't exist five or ten years ago. What we see are new industries, new jobs, and new job requirements. The most fundamental aspect of this changing environment is the fact of *change* itself, and change that seems to be accelerating! This phenomenon of change raises a profound question for curriculum builders: How can they build a curriculum to prepare students to live productive and successful lives in the future if they don't know exactly what the future will be like? What skills will the jobs of the future require people to have?

Coping With Change

One way to approach this question is to think about preparing students to cope with change. A curriculum that focuses on specific skills and rigid ways of thinking runs a high risk of teaching students soon-to-be obsolete skills. In order to cope with change, people need to be flexible in their thinking, be able to solve problems, and continue to learn new ideas and skills. Flexibility in thinking requires the understanding of ideas and the ability to see relationships and make connections among them.

The science curriculum is changing today to prepare students to survive in a world that will be very different in the next century. Although the fundamental facts and concepts of life, physical, and Earth/space sciences are still essential to learning science and are a necessary part of the curriculum, these facts and concepts are no longer sufficient in a student's science education. The appropriate sequencing and connecting of concepts both within a discipline and across disciplines are necessary to develop skills. The integration and use of basic and higher-level science process skills with conceptual knowledge is also required. These complex behaviors are necessary for the development of higher-order thinking and problem-solving skills, skills that will prepare students to live in an ever-changing society of the future. Using today's projections, by the year 2000, seven out of ten American jobs will be related to science, mathematics, or computer technology. Simply stated, if students haven't mastered science concepts, process skills and their integration as introduced in your class, they probably won't go further in science and may not have a future in a global job market.

New Curriculum Standards

In 1991 the National Research Council (NRC) was commissioned to coordinate the development of national standards for science education in grades K-12. Work on these standards is now in progress, and by 1994, National Science Education Standards will be completed and published. According to the NRC's preliminary report:

"The standards will be narrative descriptions of what all students should be able to do to engage and understand the natural world. The standards will address science curriculum, teaching and assessment and will represent the consensus of teachers and other science educators, scientists, and the general public.

The science assessment standards will define: the methods for assessing and analyzing students' accomplishments and the opportunities that programs afford students to achieve the valued outcomes of school science; the methods of obtaining appropriate correspondence between assessment data and the purposes that the data will serve;

as well as the characteristics of valid and reliable science assessment data and appropriate methods for collecting them."

These standards, while still emerging, will have a large effect on what is taught, how it is taught, and how student learning outcomes will be evaluated. Preliminary scenarios show groups of students working cooperatively on long-term projects of real importance. These groups use methods modeled on those of scientists, engineers, and technicians. Because of the complexity of these investigations, the student groups maintain descriptive journals, logs containing data bases and decisions based on them, and diagrams, drawings, and models. They engage in brainstorming and decision-making conferences, develop and present reports to other groups, and demonstrate integrated conceptual process-skill activities for observers. These activities will present numerous opportunities for alternate assessments.

Evaluating a Student's Performance
Every student of science has taken hundreds of written tests that check his or her ability to perform basic science process skills or identify specific facts. Traditional paper-and-pencil tests are the primary means used today to evaluate a student's achievement in science. And this is a natural result of a curriculum that is based on facts and basic skills. Of course, science teachers have also evaluated students' performances using other informal techniques, such as asking them to solve problems at the chalkboard, asking questions in class, or by checking their laboratory activity write-ups and homework papers. However, the pencil-and-paper test is of primary importance in evaluating students because it can be used to assign a grade.

Traditional paper-and-pencil tests are limited in what they can test. For measuring the performance of a student to use basic science process skills or recall facts, these kinds of tests can do a good job. And that is why they have been used almost exclusively in the science classroom—in the past, the curriculum has focused on teaching basic concepts and simple process skills, and not on higher-level thinking skills or problem solving. To measure a stu-

dent's ability to think scientifically, understand ideas, and solve non-routine problems in science and technology, paper-and-pencil tests are inadequate.

Testing for Improving Instruction
Another serious shortcoming of traditional written tests is their use by teachers to complete a unit of instruction by giving a test, assigning a grade, and then moving on to the next topic. Rarely are tests used as a vehicle to influence the instructional process itself. But testing and other alternate assessment techniques can and should be used to modify instruction as students progress through a topic. Assessment results can be used to change the instructional approach to a topic, priorities, examples, time, or other variables to enhance learning.

Basic concept and fact testing only shows that students can or cannot recall definitions and simple relationships. Basic process skill-oriented tests reveal only that a student demonstrates or does not demonstrate a particular skill in a pencil-and-paper testing environment. For students who cannot recall facts and basic concepts or demonstrate basic science process skills in artificial settings, there is seldom measurable value in reteaching, even if students are to be retested. This approach often produces frustration and continued patterns of failure by the student.

Goals of Instruction
The emerging standards emphasize teaching science through problem solving, integrated process skills and critical thinking skills, and looking for connections, both conceptually within science and to the real world. These standards will produce goals of instruction that cannot be fully measured using traditional paper-and-pencil tests. Students must work toward attaining these new goals on a continuous basis throughout the entire science curriculum. Basic process skill goals are discrete goals that can be measured on a piece-by-piece basis. For example, a discrete basic process skill goal is to be able to list several observations about an object or event. Students can demonstrate their ability to make observations on a paper-and-pencil test

because there is a single answer or a convergent set of answers. Once this skill is learned, further instruction on it is unnecessary.

Learning to solve problems and learning to think are continuous processes that grow each year as students master new and more sophisticated concepts, integrated process skills, and problem-solving strategies. There are no simple right or wrong answers to questions that involve these new goals.

Evaluating Goals

Process goals cannot be measured accurately by any one assessment technique. Different techniques must be used *over time* to see how students are performing on these goals. The new goals are now becoming a part of a science curriculum that is evolving to incorporate them. New textbooks and other curriculum materials that incorporate the approaches demonstrated in Scope, Sequence, and Coordination; Project 2061; and the NRC standards are currently being introduced into schools. Therefore, it is very important that teachers expand their methods of assessing students' performances. This booklet discusses various types of alternate assessment techniques and provides many practical and useful suggestions for using them in the classroom.

PERFORMANCE ASSESSMENT

Description

If written tests are no longer adequate for measuring a student's performance on the emerging goals of science instruction, then how can these goals be evaluated? What kinds of tests are needed? And who will make up the tests?

The emerging goals of science instruction can be evaluated by using multiple assessment techniques. Tests are needed that show how students actually perform tasks. If we want students to be good problem solvers, then tests of problem-solving competency must logically assess *performance* on problem-solving tasks. No paper-and-pencil test that grades an answer right or wrong can evaluate performance. For example, think about a musician, artist, basketball player, or writer. Their work is judged by a performance in a concert, a work of art, a game, or a book. These people do not take paper-and-pencil tests to demonstrate what they know—they perform!

The same standards need to apply to students studying science. If they are to become problem solvers, students must be taught how to analyze, formulate, and solve difficult and nonroutine problems, and teachers need to judge their performances as *solvers of problems.*

When students are assessed on the basis of their performance, then testing can become an integral part of instruction. A coach works constantly with his players to set goals and improve performance. The same approach can apply to teaching science. The sequence of instruction, assessment, further instruction based upon the results of the assessment, and so on is a methodology that works to improve performance.

Not only do students need feedback on their performance, but subsequent teachers and parents also need to know about a student's progress. Thus, it is essential that written records be kept. These records will be much more than a set of written grades. They will provide a comprehensive and accurate picture of a student's performance.

Types of Assessment Techniques

The types of assessment techniques that can be used for performance evaluation are already being used by teachers in classrooms today. They are generally thought of as *informal* assessment methods and are rarely used for grading purposes. However, as every experienced teacher has learned, written tests generally confirm what the teacher already knows about a student's performance.

Alternate assessment techniques consist of *observing* students working in class and laboratory settings, *evaluating* individual and group activities in the laboratory, and *asking questions* and listening to their answers. They involve student *presentations* and *extended projects. Portfolios,* written *journals,* and *logs* that list data, show and describe students' work, and document their decision-making processes are very useful techniques. Other less frequently used but viable techniques are the use of *interviews, conferences,* and *student self assessments.* All of these assessment techniques will be discussed in detail later in this booklet.

What Does a Performance Task Attempt To Do?

The purpose of a performance task is to assess what students know and what they can do. The task should be meaningful, authentic, and worth mastering. The following criteria help to define a performance task. It should:

- be aligned with the goals, objectives, and content of the curriculum.

- allow students to display their thinking and

understanding of a science experience and not just provide a single answer.

- provide an opportunity for an evaluation of the processes involved in the task.

- be realistic, interesting, and thought-provoking.

- be representative of the goal being evaluated so generalizations can be made about a student's performance.

- stress depth more than breadth and mastery more than speed.

- be more open-ended than tightly structured.

- be divergent, that is, not have one clear path of action specified at the beginning of the task.

- raise other questions or lead to other problems.

Using Performance Tasks

As a teacher of science, you are probably wondering how to go about using performance tasks. You know that good tasks take time to construct and your day is already full. Yes, all of this sounds wonderful, you think, but you may ask if you have the time to do this kind of performance evaluation.

The answer is *yes*, but you may have to modify your methods of instruction somewhat to make them more task-oriented. You need to involve students in small-group work and give them opportunities to plan their own work, as with projects or portfolios. And you will probably need to reduce your reliance on paper-and-pencil tests.

So, how can one get started using performance tasks? First, it is wise to start slowly and gradually. It is not necessary to assess each student's performance every day, nor is it feasible to do so. Also, everything that is taught does not need to be evaluated. Selectivity of topics and students will produce an effective assessment of performance on key goals over time.

The textbook is an excellent source of potential performance tasks. After students have com-

pleted an activity, you can very often assess their comprehension of the concept and/or process skills covered by having them repeat the activity with changed variables or hypotheses. In much the same way, the laboratory manual can be used to assess performance. Text problems or examples can be turned into simple performance tasks by asking a student to "Explain why such and such is true." Asking questions that probe understanding of *why* something works in science and not always *how* it works shifts the focus from convergent thinking to logical thinking and in so doing aligns the questions with process goals of instruction.

For example, a group of students is reading about simple machines. They are learning about levers, inclined planes, wheels and axles, and their components. The teacher listens to their conversation and then asks how many simple machines are in a bicycle. Within minutes, a bicycle is in the room and students are manipulating its components. Soon they are able to list two levers and four wheels and axles on the bicycle. If the teacher had not asked the question, the students would never have integrated the concepts and skills they were studying.

There are other good sources of information that can be used to construct simple and more complex performance tasks. The National Science Teachers Association publishes many excellent books and journals such as *Children and Science, Science Scope,* and *Science Teacher* that are full of good ideas and experiments. A check of your own school library may also turn up some good references. Science, engineering, mathematics, and technology related businesses and industries are the richest sources for ideas.

Evaluating Results of a Performance Task

Performance tasks, by definition, cannot be evaluated using paper-and-pencil tests. Performance tasks involve understanding of scientific concepts and procedures; they are thought-provoking, often open-ended, and seldom have a single answer. The evaluation of such tasks involves the professional judgement of a trained teacher.

Before challenging students to attempt a performance, the teacher should explain the task and give the students the criteria that will be used to judge the performance. These criteria should be in writing and well understood by everyone before student performances begin.

The first step in evaluating a performance task is to establish a system of documenting students' performances.

One versatile and effective system is the scoring rubric. A rubric is not an abstract numbering system but is a classification system that provides specific assessment guidelines for teacher and student alike. Rubrics provide formative, not merely summative, assessment, providing explicit guidelines and specific examples. If these examples and guidelines are not established, performance cannot be compared to a clearly defined standard.

To be used effectively, a particular rubric must be used at various stages throughout the assessment period. This gives students the chance to show improvement in performance. Thus, rubrics allow students and teachers to establish a partnership that uses observable characteristics to measure student performance patterns over time. Students are given credit for making progress toward a goal and are not penalized for a lack of immediate success.

Rubrics can be designed to meet individual assessment needs. They can be general, or they can be developed to measure student progress toward mastery of specific skills. See page 10 for an example of a generalized scoring rubric. Whatever rubric is used, criteria must be specific so that students know what performance is needed to reach educational goals.

Performance Standards
In any assessment of what students know or can do, there is always the question of what performance standard is being used for comparison. On written tests, a numerical score compares students to one another or to an established criterion (standard). Assessing a student's performance on a performance task, however, involves an evaluation of the student's work against the task itself. The teacher's goal in making the assessment is to be able to see intellectual growth or lack of it. Two things must exist for this to happen: first, standards of performance must be established, and second, performance tasks must be written that can be evaluated using the previously established standards.

Teachers can develop their own performance standards to judge the quality of their students' work. These standards do not have to be elaborate and, in fact, can be quite simple. For example, to evaluate students' performances in solving problems, the following levels of performance can be established.

PROBLEM SOLVING	POINTS
Creative	5
Substantial	4
Average	3
Partial	2
Inadequate	1
No Attempt	0

Developing a Performance Task
Performance tasks can be short and simple, such as asking a cogent question in class that is aimed at eliciting a thinking response, or an extended project or investigation that would demonstrate a student's performance in applying scientific models to solve real-world problems. Any performance task, however, needs to meet the criteria discussed earlier, fit within the context of what the students are studying, and be capable of providing information to the teacher about what the student knows. The best designers of specific performance tasks are teachers themselves. Teachers know their students' strengths and weaknesses best and can therefore design tasks that shed light on new knowledge or deeper understanding.

Advantages of Performance Assessment

Performance assessments permit students to compete with themselves rather than others. Through such assessments, students can gain a real understanding of what they know and what they can do. Performance assessments, unlike written tests, are not threatening. Because there are many correct answers, performance assessments can take the fear out of learning science. What student has not been fearful of speaking up in class and giving the wrong answer? Very few indeed! Taking the fear and anxiety out of the science classroom may motivate many more students to continue their study of science. They will also enjoy, learn, and use more science.

Performance assessment is not an end in itself; rather, it becomes an integral part of the instructional process and helps to guide further instruction. It is through the assessment process that students learn what activities and learning outcomes the teacher values.

Performance assessment makes school learning more relevant to students' lives and to the real world. It helps teachers focus on the really important outcomes of education, instead of teaching isolated bits of information. As students learn to become competent problem solvers, confident of their ability to think logically and communicate their ideas clearly, they will recognize that they have received an education that has prepared them for life—for life as productive citizens in the twenty-first century.

What Should Performance Assessment Do?

Although the introduction and use of performance assessment tasks in science may seem different and new to many teachers, and probably even somewhat intimidating in terms of the time and effort required to implement and evaluate them, this is not necessarily the case. Many science teachers have used performance assessment tasks for years in teaching their courses but in an informal and casual way. The time has now come to shift the focus of assessment from the exclusive use of written tests to a more balanced and realistic assessment of performance. In thinking about performance assessment tasks, teachers should keep the following ideas in mind. Performance assessments in science should:

- be introduced gradually by using some simple but useful tasks.

- focus on goals of instruction.

- be used at all grade levels.

- involve natural extensions of sound methodology for teaching science.

- not be complex and difficult to implement.

- eventually become an integral part of the assessment process.

- engage teachers in discussing the goals of instruction.

- lead to the development of sets of various assessment tasks that are aligned with the curriculum.

- lead to the development of criteria to evaluate performance tasks.

- give a realistic and in-depth understanding of what a student knows and can do.

Samples of Performance Tasks

Performance tasks in science are numerous and exist at several different levels. They are best used to allow students to demonstrate their understanding of several related concepts and process skills. Although a laboratory activity can be a performance task, it is usually a short-term task that often only replicates some model of performance and yields a right or wrong solution. Real-life performance tasks can be much more involved. They can last several weeks and result in very divergent outcomes for different students and groups of students. Consider the following scenarios for group performance tasks.

1. Your group is given two identical "milk carton" cars. One has full-width wheels. The second has had its wheel width reduced by one-half. Design an experiment to test the variable of wheel width and its effect on distance traveled. After you have designed the experiment, test each car at least three times. Record the data and analyze it. Write

a report describing your project and presenting the results.

2. Your group wants to study the effect of different amounts of exposure to sunlight each day on the growth of identical plants. Design an experiment that varies the sunlight from zero hours per day to twenty-four hours per day. Use at least four identical plants, and collect data for at least one month. Graph the data, analyze it, and write a report describing your project and presenting the results.

3. Your group is given design paper, cardboard, clay, pencils, half-gallon milk cartons, and cardboard tubes from rolls of paper towels. You are also given some model aluminum cans made from aluminum foil. The model cans are approximately one-third the size of an actual beverage can. Using principles of simple machines, construct a prototype can crusher that can effectively crush the model cans. After testing the prototype, present a demonstration and oral report to the class. Make a scale drawing of the can crusher device, and write out step-by-step instructions for its construction.

4. Your group is presented with a large number of plastic containers from consumer products, beverage cans, vegetable and fruit cans, newspaper, cardboard, magazines, and glass bottles and jars. You are also given plastic bags, twist ties, labels, a can opener, a magnet, an aluminum can-crushing device, and a plastics-recycling key. Design a system that can be used to separate, package, and store the materials for delivery to a recycling center. Based on your experience, apply your system to the school and its recyclable materials. Write a report describing the recycling system, detailing its strengths and weaknesses. Present the report to the class and the school administration.

These are only four examples, but they present the integrated process-concept approach that is found in real-life science and engineering tasks. These four examples are complex and require several days or weeks of concentrated thought, planning, and work. Each one includes a design stage followed by performance based on the design model. Finally, the results of each performance are documented and communicated in writing, through an oral report, or both. These types of integrated concept-process skill tasks involve real-life problem solving and have immediate impact on the students participating in them. The learning is involved in the process of designing, performing, and communicating. There are no single correct answers, and, like real life, the participants in these tasks often learn as much from their failures as from their successes.

GENERALIZED SCORING RUBRIC

Response	Criteria	Rating
Exemplary	Response is concise, clear, complete, and unambiguous; includes some graphic representation of data or results; shows understanding of all processes, procedures, and apparatus involved; proposes a hypothesis; analyzes results in terms of the hypothesis; draws correct inferences and conclusions from empirical results.	6
Competent	Response is fairly concise, clear, complete, and unambiguous; may include some graphic representation of data or results; shows understanding of major processes, procedures, and apparatus used; proposes a hypothesis; analyzes results; draws acceptable inferences and conclusions from empirical results.	5
Minor Flaws	Completes the assignment or experiment satisfactorily, but the explanation may be slightly ambiguous or unclear; graphic representation, hypothesis, analysis, inferences, and conclusions may be incomplete, inappropriate, or unclear; shows incomplete understanding of processes, procedures and apparatus used.	4
Nearly Satisfactory	Begins the assignment or experiment satisfactorily, but omits significant parts or fails to complete; may misuse scientific terms; graphic representation of data or results may be incorrect or omitted; incorrect or incomplete analysis, inferences, and conclusions; inappropriate or omitted hypothesis.	3
Fails to Complete	Assignment or experiment and its explanation are not clear, concise, or accurate; major flaws in concept mastery; incorrect use of scientific terms; inappropriate or omitted hypothesis.	2
Unable to Begin Effectively	Explanation, hypothesis, graphic representations, and analyses do not reflect the assignment or experiment; does not distinguish what information is needed for successful completion; copies procedures without making an attempt at solution.	1
No Attempt Made	Does not begin assignment or experiment.	0

OBSERVATION AND QUESTIONING

Description

The assessment techniques of observation and questioning are not new to teachers of science. In every science classroom, students' behavior and performance on scientific tasks are observed and students are questioned about their work. During the introduction to a new topic or a review of previously taught material, teachers use questions to check student understanding and then make appropriate adjustments in their instructional approach.

The emerging process goals of science instruction, however, imply that the techniques of observation and questioning be reexamined to make sure they are being used effectively to assess the new goals. In other words, new curriculum standards will require new or revised assessment methods.

How can a teacher evaluate a student's performance on laboratory skills or probe critical thinking and problem-solving tasks? How does a teacher assess a student's knowledge of scientific connections?

Problem Solving

Let's look at problem solving first. Traditionally, teachers assign students science problems to solve and then grade their written work on the basis of a right or wrong answer. This procedure has serious shortcomings and often reveals little useful information. For example, a student may understand *how* to solve a problem, but a misconception resulting in a wrong answer would lead a teacher to think otherwise. A more powerful way to assess problem-solving competence is to ask students questions about how they tried to solve a problem. Listening to the students' descriptions of their thinking and observing their written work provides a more accurate assessment of problem-solving skills than simply grading answers on a test.

Thinking, Communicating, and Making Connections

Questioning students in a problem-solving context reveals how they think and their ability to communicate ideas clearly. The teacher observes by listening, asking questions, and evaluating responses. Such a procedure allows the teacher to change the direction of the questions to pursue other ideas or thoughts the students may have expressed, thus getting a fuller and deeper understanding of the process being evaluated. Asking the right questions can also reveal how students make connections of what they know.

Using Open-Ended Questions

The best type of questions to ask students to assess their knowledge of science processes are open-ended questions. Such questions do not have a single answer. They allow students an opportunity to think for themselves and to demonstrate their understanding of a problem or other situation. The use of such questions can reveal a great deal of interesting information about what a student knows and understands. They also allow students to express their originality and creativity. Open-ended questions are incompatible with the erroneous notion that science consists of memorizing responses to questions that always have one right answer. Open-ended questions teach students to see and understand science as a beautiful, logical, and connected body of ideas that has great practical significance in understanding the world we live in.

Examples of Open-Ended Questions

Open-ended questions often involve the use of words such as the following:

- Describe
- Explain
- Compare
- Tell
- Analyze
- Examine
- Show
- Demonstrate
- Sketch
- Explore
- Illustrate
- Present
- Contrast
- Express
- Investigate
- Prove
- Restate
- Model
- Predict
- Operationally define

At various grade levels, a teacher can ask students:

How would you explain . . . ?
Analyze the variables . . .
Tell the class why . . .

Observing Students' Performances

Students can be observed working as individuals, in small groups, or within a whole class setting. Observations are useful for individual diagnostic purposes to determine what a student understands so remedial action can be taken, to guide students working in a small group toward the goals of the group, or for instructional feedback as students participate in class instruction.

A teacher can use the feedback to modify instruction as it is taking place to better meet the needs of the class.

Observation of students at work is a natural part of the classroom process. Very often these informal observations are unplanned, and no attempts are made to record what has been observed. However, in assessing the process standards of instruction, systematic observations are necessary to form an understanding of how well students are performing against the standards. In other words, to understand how a student solves problems, a teacher should observe closely the student's attempt to solve a problem.

The same is true for evaluating students' critical-thinking skills. This can be done by listening to students explain their reasons for their work, that is, by observing their minds at work through the use of language. Of course, written work also is read and observed and thus is significant in forming a complete picture of scientific competence.

Observations are useful in assessing performance in the following areas:

- Laboratory skills
- Problem-solving approaches
- Thinking processes
- Understanding of concepts
- Communication skills
- Working in small groups
- Making connections

Implementing Questions

Questions, like observations, are an integral part of the instructional process. In fact, worthwhile observations are often the result of asking the right question. Questions can be directed toward individual students, small groups, or the class itself. Students' responses can be used for assessment purposes, to guide instruction, or to identify errors.

Sample Questions

Let's look at some sample questions as they relate to problem solving, laboratory skills, reasoning, and connections.

Problem Solving

- Would you explain the problem in your own words?

- What is the problem about?

- Describe how you would solve the problem.

- Would making a drawing or a sketch be helpful in solving the problem?

- Explain the steps you would follow to solve the problem.

Laboratory Skills

- How could we test that idea?

- What variable will change our results?

- Write a short paragraph about the activity that you did in class today.

- Explain your solution to the problem at the chalkboard.

Reasoning

- Can you formulate a hypothesis based on the facts you know?

- Explain why the solution to the problem is incorrect.

- Why are definitions necessary in science?

- Can you generalize that result?

- What conclusions can you draw about the hypothesis from the given data?

Connections

- Can you give a practical example of the use of that concept?

- How does water speed affect organisms in a stream?

- Why is the freezing and melting of water important in geology?

- What is the connection between pollution and quality of life?

- How would you graph the data from the experiment?

- Do you see any relationship of that idea to what we discussed yesterday?

Assessment Questions

When using questions to make an assessment of what a student knows, here are some general guidelines to follow.

1. Make a list of questions in advance.
2. Allow students sufficient time to answer your questions.
3. Encourage students to make notes and ask you questions to clarify a point.
4. Record responses in an organized format.
5. Draw a conclusion about the students' responses.

Questions to Guide Instruction

During the course of an instructional period, that is, when the teacher is developing a new topic, timely and astute questions can provide significant feedback as to how well the instruction is being received. Do the students understand the main points of the presentation? Are more examples needed? Should a review be introduced to reinforce ideas and skills from previous lessons? A teacher needs to know answers to these questions and others in order to shape the instruction to the class. Without asking questions, there is no way to find out where the students are. Effective science instruction and the use of good questions go hand in hand.

Questions for Error Analysis

One of the best ways to find out why students make certain types of errors is to ask them to explain their work. Usually, students' explanations reveal a faulty understanding of some key concept or a lack of knowledge of a specific fact or procedure. An analysis of written work may not reveal the reason an error is being made. To correct persistent types of errors, they must first be diagnosed correctly and then further remedial instruction must be given. Asking questions and listening to students' answers is one of the most effective ways to identify and analyze errors.

Evaluation Methods

One of the major purposes of assessing students' work is to provide feedback regarding how well they are doing. Students need to know what the teacher thinks about their progress or lack of it. Informal assessment methods such as observations and questioning are seldom documented, but they should be if feedback is to be accurate and effective.

Given the dynamics of a science classroom and the number of students a teacher works with each day, methods of recording observations and the results of systematic questioning must of necessity be simple and easy to implement. Also, only *significant events* should be recorded. Such an event is likely to be either an atypical student behavior or a clear indication of some understanding or lack of it.

Here are three methods that can be used to record significant events.

1. Make a *class list* of your students with a column for writing comments. Or use an *observation sheet* for each student.
2. Develop *profiles* for students. Each profile can evaluate important attributes such as a student's use of problem-solving strategies, scientific vocabulary, plausible arguments, or different models.
3. Construct a *checklist* for each student of skills, behaviors, or attributes that you want to encourage.

An example of such a checklist for assessing specific laboratory skills follows.

LABORATORY SKILLS ASSESSMENT

Name_____ Date_____

Rating Scale: **1.** student is careless
2. student needs to improve
3. student is proficient

Skill	Proficiency		
lights burner correctly	1	2	3
adjusts air and gas supply correctly	1	2	3
decants correctly using a stirring rod	1	2	3
folds filter paper correctly	1	2	3
carries a balance correctly	1	2	3
determines mass accurately	1	2	3
positions thermometer correctly	1	2	3
records accurate reading	1	2	3
identifies the parts of a microscope	1	2	3
carries microscope correctly	1	2	3
focuses microscope correctly	1	2	3
inserts glass tubing correctly	1	2	3

A few suggestions for constructing and using a checklist are listed below. Remember, a checklist should be helpful and not be a burden to use.

- Focus on only a few students each day, perhaps four or five.

- Observe laboratory groups as a whole and as individuals.

- Document individual and group work.

- Use the list periodically, not daily.

- Have students review the initial list to review and make suggestions for revisions.

- Ask students to evaluate themselves, using the checklist.

- Leave space for notes.

Each evaluation method is a way of recording information about a student in order to provide feedback. Such feedback can take the form of written or oral comments by the teacher. Feedback provides a link with previous instruction and points the way to future instruction. And it tells students what learning outcomes the teacher values. Feedback equips students to monitor their own progress and work toward the goals established by the teacher.

Sample Forms

The following types of forms are illustrative of those that can be used to record information resulting from observation and questions.

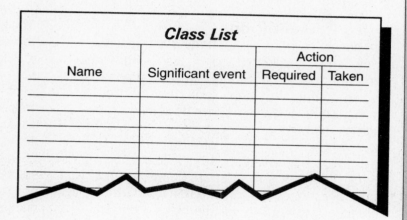

Class List

Name	Significant event	Action	
		Required	Taken

OBSERVATION SHEET

Name _____

Date	Activity	Observed behavior

Name _____ Week ____

PROFILE NOTES

PRESENTATIONS AND DISCUSSIONS

Students who might feel shy speaking in front of the whole class may be more at ease talking to a small group. Students are also less fearful of making errors when working with only two or three other students.

Why Are Presentations and Discussions Important?

What better way would a teacher be able to assess a student's ability to communicate scientifically than to hear that student give a verbal explanation to a problem or an oral report on a topic of interest in science. Certainly, no written test could perform this function by having a student make marks on a piece of paper.

Using Presentations

The use of student presentations and discussions can be a valuable tool in assessing a student's performance. Student presentations can involve oral presentations to the class or to small groups. They can either be rather simple, such as explaining observations, or somewhat more involved such as an oral report to the class. Student presentations can also involve the use of models to illustrate concepts and laboratory procedures, or the construction of bulletin board displays for the classroom. Student demonstrations of activities or safe use of scientific apparatus are also of value.

Using Discussions

Discussions involve small groups of students working together and can be teacher directed or student directed. Teachers often involve students in a discussion of new topics, although in science classrooms some students are often reluctant to participate because of fear of giving the wrong answer. As students learn science within a problem-solving context, the one-answer syndrome begins to dissipate, and they start to open up and express their ideas more freely. Also, as students grow in their ability to solve problems and think scientifically, their self-confidence grows, too. A self-confident student is not afraid to discuss ideas with classmates.

An ideal way to motivate student discussions is through the use of cooperative learning groups.

Verbal presentations and discussions are extremely important alternate assessment methods because they permit the teacher to hear what students are thinking. They also serve as a vehicle for students to present and discuss their ideas with classmates. A dynamic science classroom involves the participation of all students working together in an active mode: identifying variables, solving problems, discussing solutions, challenging assertions, and, in general, talking to one another. Presentations and discussions increase and enhance the verbal interactions within the classroom. And in so doing, they not only make the science classroom a more lively and interesting place to be, but they also make it a more fruitful teaching and learning environment.

How Can Presentations and Discussions Be Used in the Classroom?

The use of presentations and discussions must be a planned part of the instructional process. The teacher should explain to students that certain times will be used to incorporate oral presentations into the course work. Also, if students have never worked in cooperative learning groups before, they will need to be prepared for this experience. Another book in the Glencoe Science Professional Series, *Cooperative Learning in the Science Classroom*, may be helpful.

When students are asked to give a formal report or a presentation on a special topic, a mutual agreement should be reached between the teacher and student regarding the topic. Topics should be chosen that support both content goals and process goals of science instruction. Some students may need guidance in selecting a topic, but the topic should never be imposed by the teacher. This approach may destroy the student's motivation to research the topic and present it.

Small group discussions should have a focus. A very important focus is to have students engage in problem-solving activities. Different strategies can be discussed, solutions checked and compared with those of other groups, and group presentations of solutions given to the entire class. Alternative methods of solving a problem can be discussed, and models and diagrams can be used to demonstrate solutions.

Cooperative groups of students working on long-term scientific projects can maintain a simplified log. The log combines written entries such as their plan for conducting an experiment, the experiment data, and its analysis. In a six weeks' project, there may be three or four separate or related experiments. The log can then be used as a basis for a reflective student report on their project.

Suggestions for Presentations

Almost any topic that falls within the scientific maturity level of a student and the content of the course is a possibility for a class presentation. The following list is simply a source of ideas for general categories of topics.

- solution to a scientific problem
- historical topic, person, or event
- extension of textbook topic
- enrichment topic
- experimental topic
- practical application topic
- calculator or computer topic
- scientific connection topic

- scientific logic topic
- famous living scientist
- famous theory or hypothesis
- major branches of science
- scientific notation
- multicultural topic

Suggestions for Small Group Discussions

Students' work in small groups should be focused upon specific tasks. The discussions should be task-oriented, such as how to design and conduct an experiment, rather than of a more general nature. The following activities are appropriate for small group work and discussion. This list is suggestive only and is not meant to be all-inclusive.

- solving problems within areas of science and engineering
- formulating problems
- solving applications related to other disciplines or the real world
- analyzing data to support or refute theories
- using models to learn concepts or do experiments
- discussing solutions to homework problems
- classifying objects, interpreting results, generalizing solutions, making graphs
- making and testing hypotheses
- planning group presentations
- using calculators or computers
- helping less capable students through peer tutoring

When to Implement

Presentations and discussions can be used throughout the school year. If the emerging standards of instruction are to be evaluated at all, then there is really no choice but to use these alternate methods of assessment.

Instruction and assessment need to work together, however, to be successful. Thus, not only are presentations and discussions alternate assessment methods, they are also tools for instruction that can be integrated into the teaching process at any time.

How to Evaluate

Before looking in detail at how to evaluate the alternative assessment methods of presentations and discussions, let's review the purposes or goals of making an assessment. The major goal of evaluating students' presentations and discussions is to document their growth in understanding. What progress, if any, has Ann or Bill made in his or her ability to solve problems, reason and communicate scientifically, and use connections both within science and to the real world?

In a classroom that makes use of presentations and discussions, information about students' performances will be abundant. The key task for the teacher is to isolate the significant information about each student so that it can be recorded and documented. Trying to record everything students say or do is impossible and would provide no useful data. A screening device is needed to make the task of identifying areas of growth practical, simple, and educationally sound.

Identifying Areas of Growth

The emerging goals of science instruction are continuous and need to be evaluated along a continuum. A teacher needs to know at the beginning of the school year where each student is on the continuum in order to identify and record areas of growth. Once a baseline has been established, then growth can be more readily observed and recorded. How then are areas of growth observed? Growth in students' scientific understanding will be indicated by their actions in each of four key areas.

Growth in Problem Solving

A teacher should look for growth in the following areas.

- use of problem-solving strategies to understand and solve problems

- use of scientific models to identify key aspects of a situation in order to formulate a problem

- use of answers and results to problems and other scientific situations to verify and interpret them with respect to the original problem

- generalization of strategies and solutions to new problem situations

- use of problem-solving methods as a means to learning and understanding new content

- application of scientific modeling to real-world problems

Growth of Communication

Growth in these areas is significant.

- use of scientific vocabulary to explain ideas to others

- use of correct statements of definitions, laws, and theories

- use of definitions, laws, and theories to discuss, interpret, and evaluate scientific ideas

- use of scientific terms to make convincing arguments

- use of language to formulate problems, definitions, and generalizations discovered through investigations

- asking clear and concise questions and giving clear answers

Growth in Reasoning

Significant growth areas are as follows.

- use of deductive and inductive reasoning

- use of data-based arguments

- evaluation of their own thinking and others' arguments

- making and testing hypotheses

- formulating data-based generalizations

- following logical arguments

- construction of scientific models

- appreciation of the use and power of logical reasoning in science

Growth in Connections

Look for growth in the following areas.

- use of concepts and process skills to explore and solve problems

- use of one or more scientific ideas to understand other scientific ideas

- use of science to solve problems in the real world or in other disciplines

- recognition of equivalent representations of the same concept or process skill

- looking for and identifying connections within science

Documenting and Reporting Growth in Understanding

One way to document and report growth in understanding the process goals of science is by using a *checklist*. A checklist can be constructed using the areas of growth identified above. Remember, a checklist should not be a burden but should make it easy to collect and record data about students.

Another way for a teacher to evaluate students' presentations and discussions is to keep a record of significant understandings in the form of an *anecdotal report*. The compilation of such anecdotes can be used to track a student's performance and to review and write summary statements about performance. Anecdotal reports consisting of brief comments are easy to implement and can be used over time as a reservoir of data for more comprehensive reports.

A *descriptive report* also can be helpful to document and report growth in scientific understanding. Such a report will take time to write, but it can be a very effective tool in evaluating a student's progress in science. The goals of a report are to point out what the student has done well and what areas need improvement. Here are some items that can be discussed in a descriptive report.

- the work a student has done

- examples of significant scientific events

- growth or improvement in a student's work

- areas that need additional work

- participation in class and small groups

- attitude toward science

- specific suggestions for additional work

Sample Report Form

The following descriptive report form is a sample that can be adapted to meet the needs of teachers who wish to write such reports.

Report of Performance

Name _____

Time period _____

Class _____

_____

Description of work _____

_____

_____

Examples of significant work _____

_____

_____

Growth and improvement observed _____

_____

_____

Areas needing additional work _____

_____

_____

Group work _____

_____

_____

Attitude _____

_____

_____

Summary comments _____

_____

_____

PROJECTS AND INVESTIGATIONS

Description

In a skill-oriented curriculum, the use of long-term projects for instruction and evaluation of scientific growth has been very limited. In many schools, all students have been required to complete a project for the annual science fair. They are often required to use "The Scientific Method." This is usually a very formal, convergent procedure. All students are required to follow the same, lock-step process that yields remarkably similar outcomes. This type of individual student project is being replaced by long-term, cooperative group projects that involve a wide variety of concepts, basic and integrated process skills, problem identification, and solutions techniques. In a curriculum that values integrated process skills and higher order concepts, meaningful projects play a significant and integral role for all students.

Projects and investigations can involve individual students or small groups of two to four students working together. They should not be very short assignments but should involve students in an ongoing task for at least two or three weeks. Projects involving more substantial activities can last for a month or two. Since students should be involved in more than a few projects during the course of a school year, the ideal duration of a project is probably about four or five weeks.

Ideas for Projects and Investigations

Projects are a wonderful way to involve students in extended problem-solving situations. These situations may be purely scientific, but most likely they will be related to the real world and other disciplines. Projects can involve students in open-ended situations that may have a variety of acceptable results. Or they may be of such a nature that the problem situation leads students to formulate questions or hypotheses that require further investigation. Projects also provide opportunities for students to explore scientific ideas using physical materials or new technology such as electronic sensors, graphing calculators, and computers.

Projects that are embedded in a problem-solving content can be used by students to explore, study, think about, and pursue ideas that develop their understanding in all the important content areas of the science curriculum.

Real-World Projects and Investigations

Projects and investigations can teach students many connections of science to the real world. For example, at the middle school level, projects can be constructed that involve the use of science in the following areas. This is only a brief list that could easily be expanded by students working together in a brainstorming group.

- Food and fitness
- Population
- Movie videos
- Environmental problems
- Farmland
- Careers
- Cars, boats, airplanes, rockets
- Business
- Sports
- Recycling
- Travel
- Space
- Cities
- Foreign countries

Additionally, projects and investigations can make connections of science to other disciplines such as mathematics, social studies, music, economics, computers, geography, and so on. All of these activities bring science to life for students by showing them the usefulness of scientific ideas and techniques to a wide range of practical activities.

When to Implement

Students can be involved in projects and investigations at any time during the school year. You may want to wait until the first three or four weeks of school have passed before discussing the use and role of projects in the course. This will allow some time for students to feel comfortable with the course content before they pursue their first project.

The first few projects students work on should be rather simple and straightforward. You can either suggest some project ideas or ask the students to come up with their own. Many students will probably need your guidance to formulate their first plan for a project. As the year progresses, however, students should be able to work more independently.

How to Implement

You can begin by talking to students about the idea of a project and that you will be using them in the course for both instructional and evaluation purposes. Discuss the process goals of instruction—problem solving, communication, reasoning, and connections—and point out their central place in the study of science. Tell students that their projects should be problem-solving oriented and relate to the content of the course. At the beginning of the school year, the first projects students work on will most likely relate to the content of the first or second chapter of their textbook. In fact, you will probably be able to use the textbook as a source for some project ideas.

Another suggestion for a first project would be to assign students a meaningful problem to work on. Make sure, however, that it is a problem that is different from a traditional science problem such as observing the properties of a magnet. It should be a challenging problem that

students need to spend some time thinking about. As a second project, you could ask students to research and present their own non-routine problems in a student log. The log is simply a bound or loose-leaf notebook that contains the problem statement, problem solution plan, activity and experiment designs, results and data, conclusions, and preliminary and final project reports.

More Specific Suggestions for Students

In order to help students get started on their projects, you will need to share with them some specific guidelines for using the student log for formulating, researching, and presenting projects.

First, it is important that students be able to write down a clear *description* of what the project is about. The teacher should review and critique this description to make sure the student has not taken on a project of unrealistic proportions or one that is simply too difficult. The project needs to be doable and provide experiences that contribute to scientific growth of the student.

Second, the student should indicate how he or she intends to research the project. Does a hypothesis need to be stated and tested? Do measurements have to be made or data collected? Will library research suffice? Do interviews have to be conducted? Is a computer necessary? In other words, students should state what *procedures* they intend to follow in the course of working on the project.

Third, students should keep a written record of their work on the project. They should write down the purpose of the project, the procedure followed, and any materials used. They should also record any questions that arose in working on the project, keep track of data, and make notes of their thoughts and ideas about the project. They should also decide how to best communicate results; graphs, charts, tables, and so on may be used.

Last, students should write out their conclusions, questions, proofs, or whatever form their *results* take. This final report can be presented either as an oral or a written report.

The steps outlined above will help students to become successful investigators. They will also provide important documents for teachers to review in assessing the educational outcomes of the projects and shaping future projects.

Desirable Outcomes of Projects and Investigations

The use of projects in the science classroom can have many positive learning outcomes for students. In addition to developing students' scientific skills, projects provide opportunities for students to grow intellectually and socially. The following outcomes are a result of working on projects.

- learning to define problems and conduct independent research

- learning to work with others when doing a group project

- learning that real-world problems are often not simple but require extensive effort over a long period of time

- learning to see science as a practical, problem-solving technique

- learning to organize, plan, and pursue long-term objectives

- learning to correctly use scientific materials

- learning to write reports of investigations

Scientific outcomes of projects are many and varied. No one list can encompass everything that students could learn from doing projects, but a general list of outcomes can certainly be written. Projects can be of the utmost importance in developing scientific capabilities because they provide opportunities for students to do the following:

- solve and formulate problems in science and make applications to the real world

- use scientific language to communicate ideas

- use analytical skills

- use the ability to apply reasoning skills

- demonstrate knowledge of concepts, skills, and scientific theories and laws

- make connections within the sciences and to other disciplines

- develop an understanding of the nature of science

- integrate scientific knowledge into a more meaningful set of concepts

Evaluating Project Work

A teacher needs to evaluate project work by looking for evidence of the growth of scientific reasoning. If students have organized their projects according to the guidelines of this booklet, that is, if they have followed the steps of (1) writing a description of the project, (2) identifying the procedures they intend to follow, (3) keeping a written record of their work, and (4) stating their results, then an evaluation of the project is not only possible but even rather simple.

The description of the project will help the teacher identify the key scientific growth areas of the project. Of course, these relate to problem solving, reasoning, communication, and connections. The procedure to be followed should be useful in identifying more specific aspects of each growth area for evaluation. The written record and statement of results will enable the teacher to see the student's thinking as he or she has attempted to complete the project. Thinking implies understanding or a lack of it, and the written record can give the teacher insight into a student's progress in developing scientific reasoning.

Each project must be evaluated on its own merits. A written project can be used to assess a student's writing skills. If the project is presented to the class, oral communication skills can be assessed. A proof or solution to a difficult or non-routine problem provides evidence of problem-solving abilities and reasoning skills. The collection, organization, and analysis of data provide evidence of problem-solving and thinking skills also. The use of different techniques to represent or model a situation, for example, diagrams, equations, or graphs, exhibit an understanding of scientific connections. A teacher's evaluation of growth in any of these areas is necessarily somewhat subjective and is based upon an understanding of where each student is on the learning continuum. Any evaluation, of course, implies that students are informed of the teacher's assessment. Students need to know how they are performing if further growth is going to take place.

Projects can be evaluated on either a *holistic* or *analytical* basis. Holistic scoring makes judgements based on a project as a whole. For example, a teacher can read and evaluate a sample of projects to determine a range of performance. Three to five categories can be established, and as the teacher evaluates the rest of the projects, they can be placed in the established categories. After final adjustments, grades can be assigned.

Analytic scoring breaks the project down into specific elements or components and establishes point values for each one. For example, using the suggestions in this booklet, the following components and point values could be used to evaluate projects.

Element	Point Value
• Problem description	10
• Research method	10
• Project steps/Work record	20
• Data	20
• Conclusions	20
• Project report	20
• Project grade	100 points

This analytic process provides checkpoints for individuals and groups undertaking long-term projects. One advantage of analytical scoring is that it allows for checkpoints, redoing, and rewrite of the project elements. This approach allows students to receive maximum points on each element when they demonstrate mastery of the concepts and skills involved.

Projects, in general, should be broadly structured so that students can display their thinking processes and respond creatively. Teachers' evaluation of creative thinking can be expressed either holistically or analytically.

Cooperative Group Projects

The use of extended projects for the study of science and as an assessment tool to determine what students understand about science can be enhanced by having students work together in cooperative groups. These groups can function both in the classroom and out of class.

Working within a group allows students to pool their contributions to the implementation and results of the project. However, in so doing, the contributions of each individual student may be lost unless a record is kept as to who has done what. This is important when group project work is being evaluated. An evaluation should certainly be made of the group's performance, but it is equally as important to assess what each student has contributed to the group. This may be most easily done by having a written log of group activities. Roles such as investigator, materials manager, reporter, and maintenance director can be rotated among the group members. After the final group report is written, each student can participate in an oral presentation of the group's project.

Sample Forms

A log sheet such as the one shown can be used for cooperative group projects. The sheet is used to keep a record of the group's work.

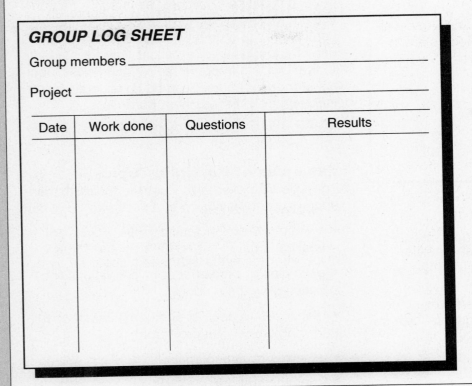

GROUP LOG SHEET

Group members _____

Project _____

Date	Work done	Questions	Results

A project record may require many pages in order to document the written record adequately. This form can help students organize their work.

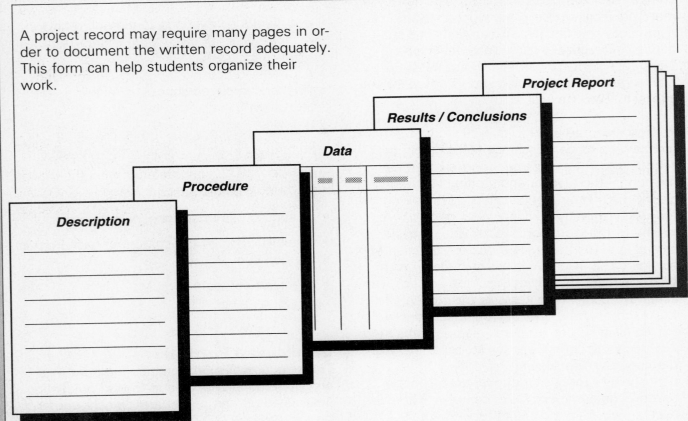

Description

Procedure

Data

Results / Conclusions

Project Report

PORTFOLIOS AND JOURNALS

Description

A *portfolio* is a representative sample of student work that is collected over a period of time. Portfolios tell a story about student activities in science. Their focus is on problem solving, thinking and understanding, written communication, science connections, and students' views of themselves as learners of science.

A portfolio is not just a folder of a student's work. The pieces of work placed in a portfolio have more significance than other work a student has done. They are chosen as illustrations of a student's best work at a particular point in time. Thus, each item in a portfolio should be dated. The range of items selected shows a student's intellectual growth in science over time.

Portfolios can be used to assess student performance on a range of science tasks during the school year. An *assessment portfolio* can be created by the teacher and student working together. At first, students collect all their work for two or three weeks in a *work portfolio.* A review of the work portfolio provides a basis for selecting items that will go into the assessment portfolio. The teacher can assist students with the review but should not direct the process. The actual selection of the items by the students tells the teacher what pieces of work the students think are significant. Student-selected items help the teacher to understand the students' views of themselves as developing "scientists." The student should submit a written reflection on the portfolio, documenting his or her growth in science during the assessment period.

A *journal* is a written account that a student keeps to record what she or he has learned. It can be used to record and summarize key topics studied, the student's feelings toward science, difficulties or successes in solving a particular problem or topic, or any other notes or comments the student wishes to make. The use of a journal is an excellent way for students to practice and improve their writing skills. Journal entries, of course, can be considered for inclusion in an assessment portfolio.

Examples of Portfolio Topics

The following examples illustrate topics that are appropriate for inclusion in a portfolio.

- a written report of an individual project or investigation

- examples of problems or investigations formulated by the student

- responses to open-ended questions or challenging homework problems

- excerpts from a journal

- scientific artwork

- a student's contribution to a group report

- a photo or sketch of physical models to illustrate a scientific idea

- teacher-completed checklists showing scientific growth

- the use of science apparatus, calculators, or computers in an investigation or problem-solving activity

- a scientific autobiography

- an applied use of science in another discipline

- an explanation by the student of each item in the portfolio

- a table of contents

Balancing a Portfolio

The selection of work samples for a portfolio should be done with an eye toward presenting a balanced portrait of a student's achievements. As a portfolio is being assembled, the major process goals need to be kept in mind and samples selected that are representative of growth in each area. Thus, students and teacher would seek samples that illustrate growth in understanding in each of the following:

- problem-solving skills
- reasoning and critical-thinking skills
- communication skills
- scientific connections

Other important curriculum considerations for portfolio samples are:

- statements on scientific attitudes such as motivation, curiosity, and self-confidence
- group skills in working with others
- use of technological tools

Advantages of Using Portfolios

The use of assessment portfolios in science has grown out of the need to align assessment tasks with emerging curricular standards and also because of the frustration and dissatisfaction felt by teachers with the narrow fact-dominated, paper-and-pencil tests. Some of the advantages of using portfolios as assessment tools are the following.

- They help to give a more complete picture of students' scientific achievement and growth.
- They emphasize complex and realistic tasks performed over a few weeks rather than speed and accuracy.
- They include students in the assessment process and encourage students' self-assessment.
- They involve students in authentic tasks of the type they will encounter outside of school.
- They motivate the study and learning of science.
- They are effective tools for teacher and parent communication about students' work.
- They encourage the development of writing skills.

Advantages of Using Journals

As students study science independently, the use of a journal can be very helpful in the development of a reflective and introspective point of view. Journal entries are conducive to thinking about why something has been done. They can be used to note questions, insights, successes, and frustrations. The use of a journal can provide a history of a student's independent work that illuminates the growth of problem-solving or thinking skills. Very often, students tend to rush through their written assignments so they can put schoolwork aside. Keeping a journal mitigates this tendency—it encourages a more thoughtful attitude toward written work and, over time, should be instrumental in helping students learn more science.

When and How to Implement

Portfolios can be used throughout the school year. If you have never used them before but want to start, and classes have already begun, it is not too late to introduce students to establishing portfolios.

You can begin by discussing the idea of a portfolio. The ideas presented in this booklet can be a starting point. You might also wish to review some other sources on the use of portfolios before your discussion with students. Go over the purpose of using portfolios and the procedures outlined below.

- Use file folders for students to collect all their work in a work portfolio.
- Ask students what they think should be included in a portfolio.
- Discuss the format of a good portfolio—neat, typed or written in ink, table of contents, personal statement as to why each piece of work was included.
- Provide variety in assignments so the portfolios can reflect this variety—group work, projects and investigations, journals, and so on.
- Have students create their first assessment portfolio from their work portfolios.
- Have students review others' first portfolios so they can see their classmates' work.

- Discuss how the assessment portfolios should be evaluated.

Discuss each student's portfolio with the student in preparation for development of the next or revised portfolio.

The initial implementation of using portfolios will be a learning experience for you as well as for your students. As you both gain experience in using portfolios, their effectiveness in guiding instruction and for assessment purposes will be increased greatly. Although the use of assessment portfolios may seem like extra work at first, their continued use will enrich the teaching and learning process.

Evaluating Portfolios

The evaluation of a student's portfolio provides an opportunity for the teacher and student to enter into a dialogue about what the student has learned. Portfolios can be assigned grades, but if the intent is to provide a judgment of the student's work, then teacher comments would be better than grades. It is possible to give all students the same grade for submitting the portfolio and meeting with the teacher to discuss its contents.

In portfolio assessment, the teacher must keep in mind that the pieces of work in the portfolio have been chosen by the students as representations of their best efforts. Thus, a portfolio is in essence a self-evaluation by the student who has created it. The teacher's goal in assessing the portfolio is to help the student gain additional insights into his or her scientific performance on the tasks exhibited in the portfolio. These insights would involve growth in the understanding of science, strengths and weaknesses of approaches and procedures, and an analysis of both the kinds of decisions made and the final outcomes of the activities in the portfolios.

Ideally, the teacher establishes assessment criteria that can be shared with the students. Thus, the criteria of establishing and assessing a portfolio is known by both the teacher and the students. It is these criteria that form the basis for the assessment comments the teacher makes on the work in the portfolio. In creating a

portfolio, the student then follows the criteria established by the teacher. Work is selected to represent the key goals of instruction.

Assessment criteria for portfolio evaluation are being established in school districts and science classrooms across the country. However, you may have to develop your own criteria. In so doing, you can develop those that are important to you and your students. The following section lists some ideas that can provide the basis for establishing your own criteria.

Assessment Criteria

The assessment criteria for a portfolio can be organized into categories that align with the curriculum goals you are trying to implement. The implementation of any set of criteria will involve the judgment of the teacher and can be holistic or analytic. The holistic judgment approach of evaluating a student's work would look for the overall quality of a piece of work in contrast to specific information or "right" steps being followed. You can also give a fixed grade for completing the portfolio process. In this mastery approach, students have the option to redo certain elements of the portfolio in order to gain all possible points.

Assessment criteria would help to guide the teacher in making holistic judgments about students' work. They would also be very useful in keeping the teacher's assessments of different students consistent.

Problem-Solving Criteria

Problem-solving criteria can be used to evaluate a student's performance in the following areas.

- understanding of problems

- use of various strategies to make a plan for solving problems

- ability to carry out a plan using models or technology

- analysis of results including statistical procedures

- formulation of problems

- creativity of approaches to complex problems

Language Criteria
These criteria apply to students' use of language to express themselves scientifically.

- use of correct terminology
- writing clearly to express ideas
- good organization of written work and journals
- explanation of results
- summary of key topics
- reflection on scientific ideas
- asking questions

Reasoning Criteria
Reasoning criteria aid the teacher in commenting on the following.

- identifying variables
- making hypotheses
- conducting an inquiry
- documenting results

- analyzing results
- critiquing ideas and procedures
- constructing, extending, applying ideas

Other Criteria
These criteria involve the following.

- relating science to the real world
- making connections within science
- development of positive attitudes
- valuing of science
- use of self-assessment and self-correction of work
- group work
- use of different scientific representations or models
- interpretation of ideas
- technology
- concepts and procedures

Sample Form

The following sample form can be used to write assessment comments for a student's portfolio.

Assessment of Portfolio

Student _____

Teacher _____

Date _____

1. Concepts, procedures, process skills explored _____

_____

_____

2. Areas of growth in understanding _____

_____

_____

3. Unfinished work or work needing revision _____

_____

_____

4. Assessment of the following areas:

    a. Problem-solving work _____

_____

_____

    b. Reasoning and critical thinking _____

_____

_____

    c. Use of language _____

_____

_____

    d. Other _____

_____

_____

OTHER TYPES OF ALTERNATE ASSESSMENT

Description

In addition to the major models of assessment discussed in the previous sections of this booklet, the following assessment techniques also can be used to monitor students' performances:

- Interviews and Conferences
- Student Self-Assessment
- Student-Constructed Tests
- Homework

Each of these other types of alternate assessment methods is discussed in the following sections.

Interviews and Conferences

Interviews and conferences provide an opportunity for the teacher and student to meet together to discuss science. This personal meeting with a teacher can be a powerful motivating experience for many students. It can also provide the teacher with a great deal of useful information about how the student thinks and feels about science.

An *interview* can be structured around questions that relate to a specific scientific topic. For example, a problem-solving interview would pose a problem for a student to solve. Working from a planned set of questions, the teacher is interested in learning how the student goes about solving the problem. The student explains his or her choice of models and strategies to solve the problem, the procedure followed, and the meaning of the solution. Questions by the teacher and verbal responses by the student are key ingredients of an interview.

A *conference* is not quite as focused as an interview. A conference is an informal discussion involving the teacher and one student. Although a conference should always have a reason for being held—say, for example, to review and discuss a student's portfolio—it need not stay with that purpose exclusively. Let the students talk, ask questions, and discuss what is important to them. Appropriate comments and questions by the teacher can elicit valuable assessment information from the student that may be impossible to get in any other way.

Helpful Hints for Interviews and Conferences

The following helpful hints have been suggested by the National Council of Teachers of Mathematics. They are also useful in science.

- Be ready ahead of time with questions.
- Put students at ease.
- Explain that you are looking for creative thinking.
- Pose a problem.
- Take notes.
- Be a good listener.
- Be nonjudgmental.
- Do any instruction intervention in a separate setting.

Student Self-Assessment

One of the real benefits of using performance assessment tasks is the opportunity to have students take part in the assessment process. When assessment is viewed as an integral part of the instructional process, its focus shifts from giving tests to helping students understand the goals of the learning experience and the criteria for success.

Implicit in all alternate methods of assessment is the idea that these methods can work most effectively when students know the goals of instruction and the criteria for measuring success against those goals. Knowing the goals and the criteria for success equips students to monitor their own progress.

Encouraging Self-Assessment

In order to help students learn how to monitor their own progress, the teacher needs to explain the goals of instruction and the criteria for evaluating performances against the goals. The major instructional goals for the year can be displayed in the classroom and copies given to each student. How students will be judged on their work also needs to be discussed. Students need to understand that right and wrong answers are not a central concern. Evidence of signs of growth in understanding and of the ability to think, communicate, and solve problems are new criteria for success in science.

Encourage students to question their own work, strengths and weaknesses, accomplishments, work habits, goals, and attitudes. Ask students periodically to tell you what they have done that shows progress toward achieving their goals. Ask them also to evaluate their own reports, journals, portfolios, and so on and to provide evidence for their evaluations. All of these methods can help students learn how to assess their own work.

Using Self-Assessment Forms

One device that can be used for self-evaluation is called a self-assessment form. You and your students can design such a form together. Then, every three or four weeks students can complete the forms and give them to you. Typical questions on the forms are as follows.

- What new understanding of science have you learned recently?

- What topic is causing you difficulty at this time?

- Have you found any new topics that really interest you? Describe them.

- What do you enjoy or not enjoy about working in groups?

- How do you feel about science now?

- What progress do you think you have made in science during the past few weeks?

- What can we do to improve our science class?

Goals of Self-Assessment

As students take a more active part in assessing their own work, they will become more mature and responsible learners. Self-assessment leads to self-direction, learning how to work and think independently, learning to set goals and priorities, and learning to work hard to achieve success on school tasks and real-life tasks. These are the ultimate goals to which self-assessment can lead.

The goals of self-assessment in learning science are more modest than those stated above, but no less important. Through self-assessment, students take part in the instruction process by evaluating their own performances. Their subsequent actions should result in learning more science, correcting errors or misconceptions, improving their performances on more challenging tasks, and gaining deeper insights into the nature of science itself.

Student-Constructed Tests

An interesting idea for assessment is to have students take some tests constructed of student-made test items. For evaluation of basic skills and of factual knowledge, written tests are still an effective means of assessing performance. Having students construct their own test items gives them a sense of participation in the assessment process. They enjoy making up the items and are generally very interested in the solutions.

A class can be divided into small groups of three or four students each to make up test items. Obviously, the items need to represent the content being studied. The teacher chooses items from each group to include on the test. It is important that all students contribute to the test. If necessary, some items may have to be edited, but the essence of the item should be retained. When discussing the correct responses, contributing groups can offer study suggestions for their test items.

Another technique to add variety and interest to written tests is to have students work on *take-home tests*. This is done by some college teachers, but is not usually implemented by teachers of middle and high school students. Take-home tests can challenge students with more open-ended questions or non-routine problems. Time is not a factor as students can use all the time they need to do the test. Take-home tests can be teacher- or student-constructed.

Practical tests that cover topics from biology, geology, physics, chemistry, and other science fields offer yet another way to modify the test-taking regimen. These tools make use of physical materials to have students answer questions or perform various tasks. They can be teacher- or student-constructed and can be administered to individuals or small groups of two or three students.

Homework often is assigned and gone over in class the next day, but in most science classes it usually has no significant role in assessing a student's performance. However, this does not have to be the case. Some teachers have had success with assigning fewer homework papers but requiring that the assigned homework be completed and included in a work or assessment portfolio. Certain carefully selected homework assignments could be reviewed and evaluated on a periodic basis. Skill types of problems or exercises could occasionally be included for evaluation; however the emphasis should be on thought-provoking questions. Thus, homework can play a more important role as an alternate assessment technique.

SUMMARY

Why Alternate Assessment?

The science classroom has always been dominated by one method of testing, namely, paper-and-pencil tests that measured a student's recall of factual information and basic process skills. Today, the science curriculum is evolving to include broader, integrated process goals of instruction, such as teaching students that science *is* solving problems. The emerging goals also involve speaking, reading, writing, critical thinking, and reasoning, and are intimately connected to the real world. Alternate assessment methods are necessary to measure students' performances against these emerging goals of science instruction.

What is Performance Assessment?

Underlying the idea that paper-and-pencil tests are not sufficient for measuring a student's performance on goals that require understanding of information, and not just its recall, is the more fundamental notion that you can find out what a person knows by having the person do something. The skills of a baseball player are not judged by giving him a written test on the rule book. Rather, he is given a ball, glove, and bat and put on the field to play ball. Then an assessment can be made of his performance as a player.

The same idea applies to education. The skills and knowledge of a student as a solver of problems cannot be judged by having the student solve contrived word problems on a written test that have a single simplistic answer. Problem solving is a complex task that is based upon an understanding of concepts, strategies, experience, attitudes, and skills that develop and grow over time. In order to find out what a student knows about solving problems, tasks must be devised that allow the student an opportunity to demonstrate performance. Performance assessment is a method of assessment that attempts to find out what students know and can do by using performance tasks.

How Can I Find Out What Students Know Without Giving Tests?

No one is suggesting that written tests not be used in the science classroom. Such tests are very useful in assessing concept objectives, and clearly, concept understanding is an essential aspect of learning science. But concept knowledge alone, without the ability to solve problems, communicate scientific ideas, and see relationships, is totally useless knowledge. It will be forgotten in time and will never be put to use in the world outside of school.

Teachers can find out what students know by listening to them answer questions, by reviewing their projects, by having them give presentations and work in cooperative learning groups, and by keeping journals and portfolios. In other words, students can demonstrate what they know through a variety of performance tasks that can be as simple as answering an open-ended question or as involved as creating a portfolio. Each of these alternate assessment techniques has been discussed in detail in this booklet.

Do I Have to Make Any Changes in My Teaching?

Perhaps. Alternate methods of assessment involving performance tasks are not intrusions into the classroom; they are an integral part of the instructional process. Instruction does not end when a performance task is given, which is usually the case with a written test. The use of performance assessment tasks implies that some changes may have to be made in the way a classroom is run and organized. These changes can be introduced gradually, such as using cooperative learning groups or getting students involved in creating portfolios. Over time, however, a performance-based approach to teaching will have the effect of increasing students' participation in the learning of science and decreasing the amount of time you spend giving instructions.

Are Grades Assigned to Performance Tasks?

Grades in school are still a fact of life. Numerical assessments can be made and grades assigned to the results of performance tasks. However, since the goal of performance assessment is to judge growth in understanding, this is best indicated by a teacher's comments rather than a grade. A grade gives students the message that the work is done successfully, partially, or unsuccessfully. A teacher's comments can give a student some insight into what she or he knows and thus provide a basis for future work. Written tests and grades chop up teaching and learning into small discrete pieces of information. Performance tasks and teachers' written evaluations of them recognize that teaching and learning are continuous processes—a journey—that involve teachers and students working together toward common goals.

How Do I Get Started?

This booklet provides ideas and suggestions for using alternate assessment techniques in the science classroom. Each teacher, however, will need to use these suggestions in his or her own way to meet local goals and curriculum objectives. The National Committee on Science Education Standards and Assessment is currently working on goals, standards, and assessment in science. They will be published in the next few years. Mathematics educators have recently completed this task for mathematics and are now implementing a new set of goals and standards. We borrow some useful advice on how to get started from the 1991 NCTM Booklet entitled *Mathematics Assessment: Myths, Models, Good Questions, and Practical Suggestions.*

- Don't try to do it all at once. Start with one idea, then try another.

- Don't try to do it all alone. Involve other teachers, parents, and administrators.

- Get involved in science networking, especially through science organizations.

- Talk with others about the changes you are making. Let parents, students, and other teachers know what is happening.

- Communicate with business and industry for practical ideas about real-life assessment practices.

BIBLIOGRAPHY

Airasian, P. W. (1991). *Classroom Assessment.* New York: McGraw-Hill, Inc.

American Association for the Advancement of Science (1989). *Project 2061: Science for all Americans.* Washington, DC: American Association for the Advancement of Science.

Arter, J., and Spandel, V. (1992). "Using Portfolios of Student Work in Instruction and Assessment." *Educational Measurement: Issues and Practice,* 11, 1: 36-44.

Barnes, Lehman W. and Marianne B Barnes (1991). "Assessment, Practically Speaking. How Can We Measure Hands-on Science Skills?" *Science and Children,* 28, 6:14-15.

Carin, Arthur A. (1993). *Teaching Science Through Discovery.* New York: Merrill.

Champagne, A. B., Lovitts, B. E. and Clinger, B.J. (1990). *Assessment in the Service of Science.* Washington, DC: American Association for the Advancement of Science.

Gronlund, N. E. (1993). *How To Make Achievement Tests and Assessments.* Boston, MA: Allyn and Bacon.

Ham, Mary and Dennis Adams (1991). "Portfolio Assessment. It's Not Just for Artists Anymore," *The Science Teacher,* 58, 1:18.

Kulm, G. and Malcom, S. M. (1991). *Science Assessment in the Service of Reform.* Washington, DC: American Association for the Advancement of Science.

National Research Council. (1992). *National Science Education Standards: A Sampler.* Washington, DC: National Research Council.

Raizen, Senta A. et al. (1989). *Assessment in Elementary Science Education.* Colorado Springs, CO: The National Center for Improving Science Education.

Stiggins, R. J. (1987). "Design and Development of Performance Assessments." *Educational Measurement: Issues and Practice.* 6,3: 33-42.

Vermont Department of Education. (1992). *Looking Beyond "The Answer": The Report of Vermont's Mathematics Portfolio Assessment Program, Pilot Year 1990-1991.* Montpelier: Department of Education.

Wiggins, G. (1989). "A True Test: Toward More Authentic and Equitable Assessment." *Phi Delta Kappan,* 70, 9: 703-713.